PASSION

By Jonquille

Copyright © 2009 by Jonquille
Author Jonquille
Cover design by Deion George
Book design by Deion George
All rights reserved.
No part of this book may be reproduced in any form or by any electronic or mechanical means including information storage and retrieval systems, without permission in writing from the author. The only exception is by a reviewer, who may quote short excerpts in a review.

To order additional copies of this book, contact
Jonquille at www.emotionalenergy.us
Printed in the United States of America
First Printing: January 2011
ISBN: 978-0-692-01234-5

Passion Contents

4	Dedications	49	Vingt Et Un
5	Introduction	51	Vingt-Deux
7	Zero	53	Vingt-Trois
9	Un	55	Vingt-Quatre
11	Deux	57	Vingt-Cinq
13	Trois	59	Vingt-Six
15	Quatre	61	Vingt-Sept
17	Cinq	63	Vingt-Huit
19	Six	65	Vingt-Neuf
21	Sept	67	Trente
23	Huit	69	Trente Et Un
25	Neuf	71	Trente-Deux
27	Dix	73	Trente-Trois
29	Onze	75	Trente-Quatre
31	Douze	77	Trente-Cinq
33	Treize	79	Trente-Six
35	Quatorze	81	Trente-Sept
37	Quinze	83	Trente-Huit
39	Seize	85	Trente-Neuf
41	Dix-Sept	87	Quarante
43	Dix-Huit	89	Quarante Et Un
45	Dix-Neuf	91	Quarante-Deux
47	Vingt		

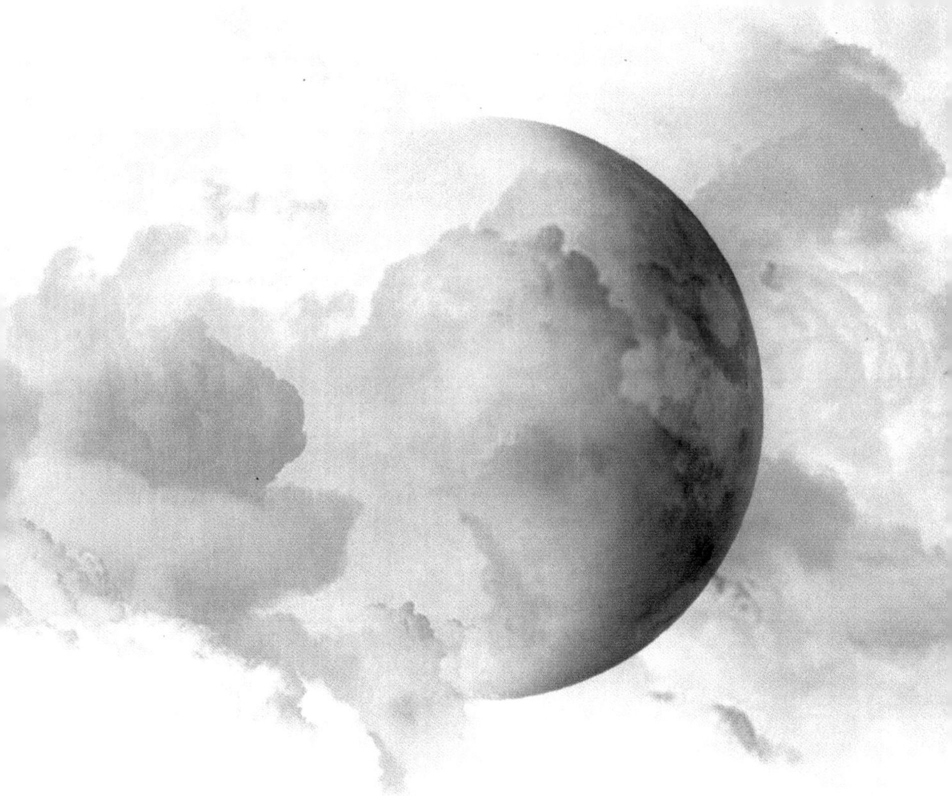

DEDICATIONS

During my travels I missed my husband immensely and out of that longing to be with him came passion. To my husband Mark and our children, I deeply appreciate and love you with every fiber of my being. Special appreciation to Deion George, Stephen George and all contributors to this publication. To all those that have inspired me and expressed to me their passion of love, want and the highs and lows of our emotions.

The first six poems are dedicated to Rev. Dwight and Mrs. Renee Turner who celebrated the passion of love, beyond our earthly realm. Thank you Renee for showing me that what I do is truly bringing words to life.

INTRODUCTION

A book of prose for those in love and those wishing to be in love. Oh, to be swept away on a cloud of dreams and fantasy. To experience the true meaning of unconditional love in its most meaningful and physical form. To experience boundless love and ecstasy. To know that you are queen not for a day, but always cherished by your king; and your king, always cherished by you. Passion to make your very being, your very core shudder with delight and desire.

The author takes you on a journey of adventure and wonderment unsurpassed by none. You are allowed to let your desires and thoughts take wings; and then you are swept away in a sea of lust and passion, only to be brought back to reality by being allowed to question your own self-fulfillment and understanding of love and passion.

You share the good times and the bad; you share memories of things past and present, and you grow even closer and stronger by your experiences. But yet, you question your actions. You question your love. You wish you could be rid of it. It hurts so much. Each step of your life's journey is a chapter bathed in admiration, self-doubt and wonderful memories.

A must read for those on the journey and those wishing and hoping to be on the journey!

Stephen George

ZeRO

A
whisper A tear A moment Silence
Together You're not alone

UN

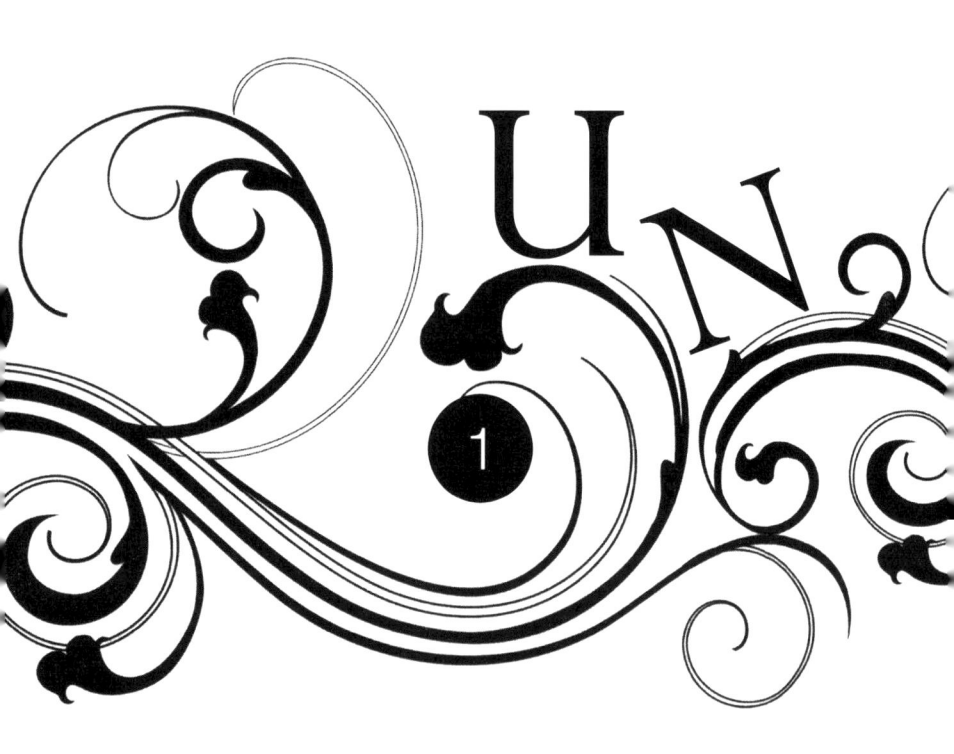

1

Let me kiss you
From head to toe
Even
In between those
Let my fingers roll
And touch
Where
Your, who knows
Let me roam
Let me explore
Let me love you
Baby

2 Deux

Hold my hand Let me take you on a journey One that will make All your dreams come true Allow me to show you the way You should be treasured Let me be your guide Through the good and the bad For you, You are my Princess Always

Trois

3

Step up onto my feet Let's waltz down that path together Watching you makes my heart smile Get ready Put on your best For this dance has just begun We will learn Respect, love, understanding and more No need to worry If you fall I'll catch you, I'll support you Let's hold hands I'll keep you close So never fear With time you'll grow And go from a Princess to a Queen

4

Quatre

You
have been
my light, my joy, my
voice, my soul I rejoice each
time we meet Where grace
has kissed my face You give me
life So that I may bask in your
essence Livin in the colors
The colors of your
world

Cinq

My love for you continues Although you're not here The mind is so powerful That I find myself with you At all times I imagine the good times And the fun things we did And suddenly my heart skips a beat I get that urge that never ceases To take you in my arms And just run I've never stopped loving you

5

5

I just love holding your hands It feels like I'm touching a rainbow And floating with the clouds Hugging you is like hugging a heart When I dream I dream of you my love Being with you makes my heart smile I love you sweetheart I know that you are proud of me And that you'll always be there for me My love

Six

6

Sept 7

Allow
me to take care of you
To stroke your hair
As you have lifted me
To wash your feet
For you have raised
me to be Caring, loving
Your peacefulness and stern
attitude Have grounded
me Allow me to give
back Just a little of
what you've given me
For I cannot even begin
to repay you You are my
heart You are my soul You
are my
forever more

Will you forgive me? That's what he asked Although the signs read Danger Keep out Still I proceed Lost, lost within you Your scent cries out Calling, pulling me Deeper and deeper So deep that I can't let go Should I, can I Forgive you Yes, oh yes For I want to be free Forget, forget no Cause I love and adore me

J it 8

When you hurt My heart breaks When you cry My soul cries When you smile I see rainbows I love to watch you sleep For I'm at peace I love to hear your laughter Which lights up the skies I love to watch you dance For my eyes dance too And listen to the sound of your voice For my body trembles with excitement I love your scent And rubbing my nose against yours Licking your luscious lips makes my heart skip a beat All that and more makes me want you Evermore

9

Neuf

DX 10

I've watched you grow in my shadow My spirit beside yours Energetic and playful Your heart beats within my heart I feel your joy and pain As you grow I shall walk with you On the path to move from prince to king Ruler of your own domain Your independent spirit is the marking of A just, upright and righteous king I am proud of you and will always be there for you For you shall be king among kings

onze

11

I

love me From the root of my hair To the tip of my toes From the way my curls grow To the fact that I can wear an afro Wherever, whenever, whatever I love me From the gray that glistens on my cornrows To the way my toenails Stops the show To the fact that the hair on my leg grows I love me From the brown in my eyes To the tone of my caramel skin I love me From my supple lips To every knee nick I love me From the width of my nose To the way my hips flow I love me From the hair on my chin The rings in my neck To my bumps and you know I love me My only flaw to me is how my belly rolls Still I love me

Douze 12

You deserve it You Mocha, Caramel, Vanilla, Ebony Queens You come in many flavors So unique that you cannot be duplicated An amazing mix That embodies the essence of a Queen And rightfully so You take your place at center stage Adorned with jewels, perfumes and A smooth silky covering protecting that skin You deserve it; shine my Queen Do you! For I long to be a Queen too

tReize
13

Thank you my love You are my precious gem You bring warmth to my soul You are my air my light My true meaning for existence You have captured my heart And much more I have requested a King From the highest order in the land He has granted my request So I say, thank you my love The most high has blessed and graced us With a most precious gift That of love

Do you remember the times we had? How much we adored each other There was a time I headed the list When love was measured No love could be equal to Or surpass ours Now we're separated And have formed a friendship One that is infinite Live, love and give thanks baby

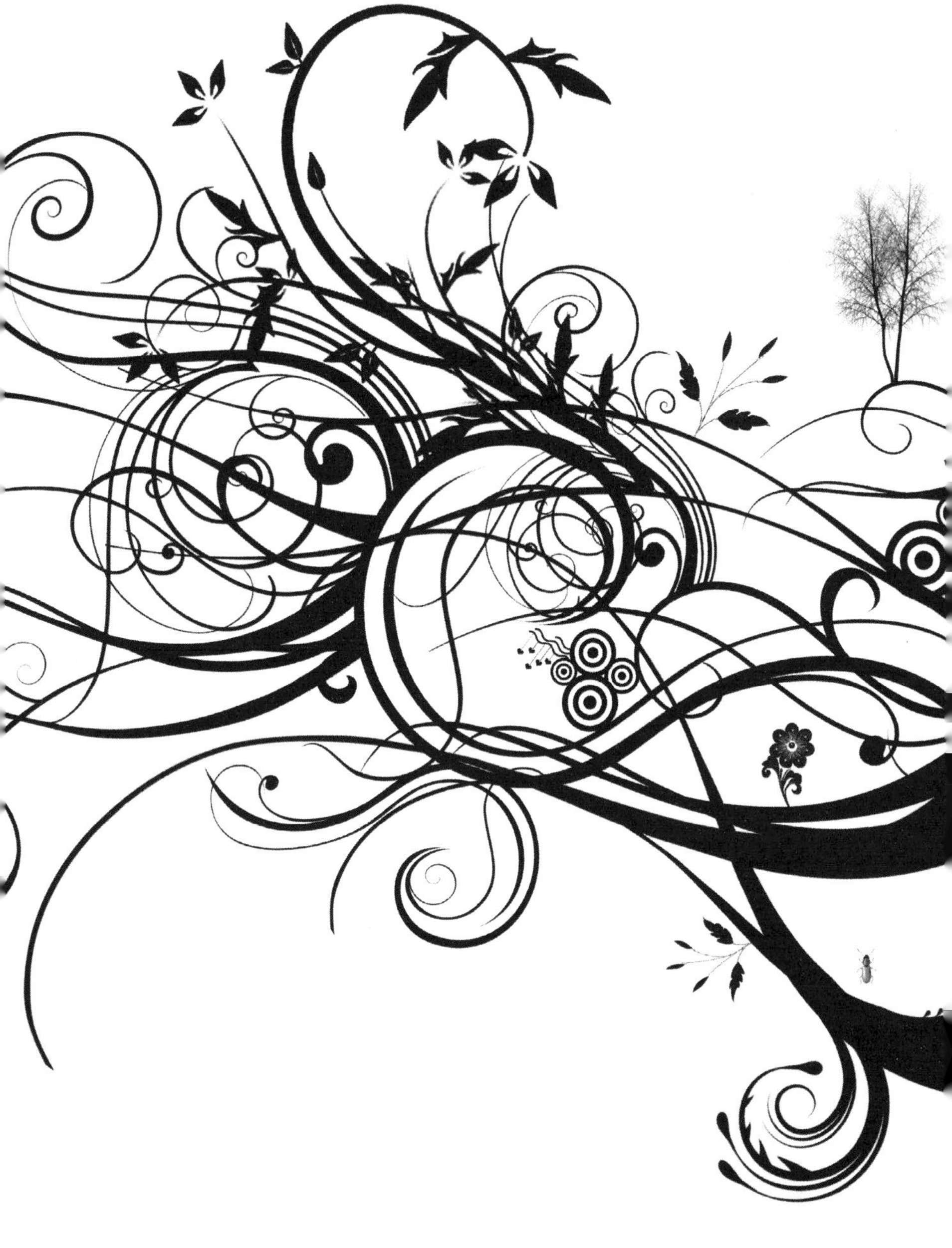

Quinzi 15

The construction of me is done daily As a carpenter constructs a home for all to see A cleansing of the soul and skin Massaged with oils and perfumes To protect from the forces around and within In preparation for my day to begin I then place my armor on given And finally my crown My crown is my glory As I step out My crown symbolizes royalty My crown completes me Adorned with jewels, shimmering For all to see Royalty, my crown my glory

16
eize

We've traveled afar and through many life times Then by chance we meet unexpectedly With one glance we know As I looked into those gleaming brown eyes and experienced that smile I knew We took a chance and found bliss We felt connected in so many ways We just wanted to revel in this moment of being Let's just continue to guide and protect each other So that we may have a fulfilling life Allow us the sense of knowing That each one is at peace Forgive yourself, as I have forgiven you We have no right to pass judgment Our paths have been set we have a second chance When the time comes you'll take me home To where we first existed in another place another time We will not be together as mates but our souls always will Be connected as one Soul mate

MATURED ONLY

I can feel within you The shock the pure energy The flowing power that forms your image Your vibe is all intense Drawing me close to you So strong, so pretty, so honest And yet the mind is not fulfilled Complete with understanding This is your ticket to be On a voyage of understanding

Dix
17
Sept

MATURED ONLY

Dix huit 18

King, uhmmm Sooooo big, Soooo commanding How I longed for you Free to roam and enjoy our adventures A King hummm! Such a deserving name Built to keep us apart in any game At times we're joined by many who yearn for Adventure too But a queen yes is much delight To feel, to touch without a flight How I yearn for you at times At day and at night The king speaks of great travels Of lovers with dreams of getting to the middle At night I set sail and after finding you We're complete coming The battle is a strong embrace until we part Single, Single calls from beyond But that's such a lonely place Ripping and running to finish the race Dreams of king begin to call, The battle begins and by morn I'm in Timbuktu and you, you're in Prague Oh, Queen how I long to be between your sheets Never alone will I be For you keep us near and force us to feel Touching, loving even if it's just feet.

Dix Neuf

In church we meet A date you'll not get A friendship yet to talk To be kept A tough of war A concession we sought A date was set After moments kept Pleased they were to laugh to talk As time went on a wife he sought An agreement was made On their own words So a bride he found and thought A preacher was he so honorable she felt But just a farce as time did tell A man whom sought control But not to control her He failed to agree In her coming in and going out She had to report without a doubt She had no time to think or breathe He had taken all she needed Now how can she live without the feel of freedom? Liberty to think, to feel Then one day while giving thanks to the lord She made an announcement That would surely get a nod Instead she felt pain and sadness Of an unstable man Now labeled as a liar and a cheat She could no longer live With a man of deceit The time had come, The hell of living with him was no longer within

MATURED ONLY

Vir

Sweetheart, He call me sweetheart And suddenly the sun came out The flowers began to bloom the sky opened up With just one word He called me sweetheart He called me sweetheart and my insides Just jumped for joy, Fireworks sparked A sense of jubilee I wanted to celebrate, I wanted to shout I wanted to dance He called me sweetheart It was not just the word but the way he expressed it With such passion, love and care As though I've never heard it before He called me sweetheart He made my body tingle My hair stand on end And made my heart skip a beat With just one word He called me sweetheart I just jumped out of my skin But I couldn't let him see my elation, my jubilation How warm I felt and whatever else He said meant nothing I heard nothing, but the fact that He called me sweetheart And it was someone that sits beside me in a pew, A stranger, a stranger besides me in a pew He called me sweetheart

MATURED ONLY

Sometimes I can't tell what you're feeling Only when you hold my hand Kiss me and come in me Sometimes I can't tell Only by the look in your eyes When it meets mine Lick those luscious lips Or your infectious laughter Sometimes I can't tell Only with your gentle touch Your smile, your soft voice, your warm embrace Sometimes I can't tell Only by the way you dance, walk and kind gestures Sometimes I can't tell Only with I do too, your wise words Sometimes I can't tell I love you

Vingt et Un

21

MATURED ONLY

Vingt Deux
22

When I look at you I can see the carefree child inside Who loves adventure? True it's been covered By fast paced growth and relationships The light breaks out and shines As a beacon in the night Come rescue me Come find me Come listen and understand me That honest smile of strength That has developed from past troubles The caring nature, the stick in the fire The longing for a resting place Be nice and kind to me As my soul is loving and my desire is happiness

MATURED ONLY

Vingt Trois 23

Teased in the afternoon, Pleased in my dreams An unexpected call, a longing The beginning of foreplay That has never been experienced A gift to give a token to receive An Adonis, an arousing seduction A planned stimuli A ring was presented, not just any ring But, one that would elicit ultimate pleasure A ring to treasure He placed it on his thunder Adorned by a beautiful marble collection Only to remain for this adventure As I unwrapped this gift I felt the heat that emanated From this gorgeous image Proclaimed the captain "Don't worry this will be a pleasure, Watch and enjoy the ride" As he began to unwind, I stroked and fantasized Of feeling it rub against my breast and mouth My heart was in his hand The ring was pulled tightly around And what was revealed was not to ponder But at the end of that thunder was The ring surrounding this luscious, juicy Hunk of meat that screamed eat As I touched and closed my eyes My mind went into a trance Wanting, needing, jumping, pouncing The heat that exuberated form That thunder made me Sweat and shake my feet I held on for the journey Was too wild to let go At the point of no return When the trip was over he left his mark I wanted to savor it Never wanting to get rid of it Seduction in the afternoon By a ring not just any ring But one that would elicit the ultimate high

MATURED ONLY

I can see what will happen To you before it does my love I cannot explain this passion that I feel I should let go for fear of hurt and pain But I can't I feel drawn, obligated, safe, bounded How can this be? The path you've chosen screams of loss for me Gains for you and that's my fear If it is so that we are bonded Tied spiritually brought together By some divined purpose I need to be your friend Your confidant, you queen, your forever I shall receive and accept whatever happens Based on prior knowledge The trust that we have in each other Our bond I believe will not be broken No matter what path we take in life I pray that you find the happiness you seek

Vingt 24 Quatre

It was your voice Your voice that soothed me And made me whole It was your voice That brought me into your world It was your voice That gave me tranquility It was your voice Taking me on that journey Your voiceeeee, your voiceeeee your voice Strong, captivating, voice Pulling me into that black hole Taking me where it's beyond my control Swooning, curing me of all my thoughts Leaving me in limbo It was your voice Your voiceeeee, Your voiceeeee, Your voice That awesome, luscious sound Such succulent sounds to ever bestow my mind Making me sweat, Making me wet Making me lose all sanity That sound, that voice Making me comeeee, Outtttt Of my skin wantingggg Needingggg, Pleadingggg Don't, stop That voice, your voice It was your voice

Vincent
25 in 9

voice........ your voice Strong, captivating, voice Pulling me into that black hole Taking me where it...
...e tranquility It was your voice Taking me on that journey Your voice..... your

MATURED ONLY

VinSix
26

The first time that I heard you I was in awe! You were so smooth That I wanted to have just a piece of what you had. You eased me into your world So incredibly smooth that it sounded Like you where weaving a web. One that I could be a part of, But it wasn't just that, It was your presence, your diction, The way you held your head high And tilted at each pause So that your audience should take notice. Your gestures, the pitch And rate of your sound Soulful voice in all the right places Blew my mind It made me stop and take notice Your strength, your voice.

I expressed to you my desire And how stoned I was on you How can I have you How do you want me to do you Fulfill my dream you said My dream of two Let me watch you Bound me, tie me, whip me Entertain me while I watch two of you Make my dreams come true I did willingly for I want you

VinGt
27 Sept

MATURED ONLY

I just love the way you touch me The way you run your hands along my body The way you kiss me The way you run your tongue all over me You don't even have to penetrate me Just touch me I just love the way you touch me The way you rub your nose against me The way your hands stroke my cheeks Ever so gently You don't even have to penetrate me Just touch me I just love the way you touch me The way your fingers go through my hair The way you whisper in my ear The way you rub my toes The way you touch those You don't even have to penetrate me Just touch me I just love the way you touch me

Vingt Huit
28

MATURED ONLY

What I really want is A chest to bury my head in A strong warm hug A hand I can hold A tender kiss A lip I can suck A head I can rub An ass I can squeeze A good toss in the back seat of a car What I really want is One that's not afraid to give love and be loved One that fills me up and I fill up on sight One that has strong moral and spiritual values One that believes in family and gives 100% One that believes in the uplifting of self and each other Long walks anywhere Slow dances whenever and wherever A rose just because A financially strong supportive man One that I can do the same for That's what I really want Can you fulfill those wants?

Vingt 29 Neuf

TreNt 30

Trapped in a love that once was How can one be so blind? With messages of hate on each side I allowed myself to be put down Stepped on, spat on, hit on Kicked, cut I allowed myself to be no more Trapped in a love that once was How can I have been so blind? With messages of love coming from above Come to me a voice said I shall heal you I shall comfort you I shall make you whole I shall remove the mask, the pain I allowed myself to be revealed through love That once was Renewed through a love that was always there

TreNte et Un
31

I love caramel in the sun Umh! How it makes you glisten Good enough to eat, what a treat As I watch you glow And darken so pleasingly That I can devour You on sight Carmel in the sun Makes my mind go places It's never been Beautiful, inviting, caramel I love caramel in the sun

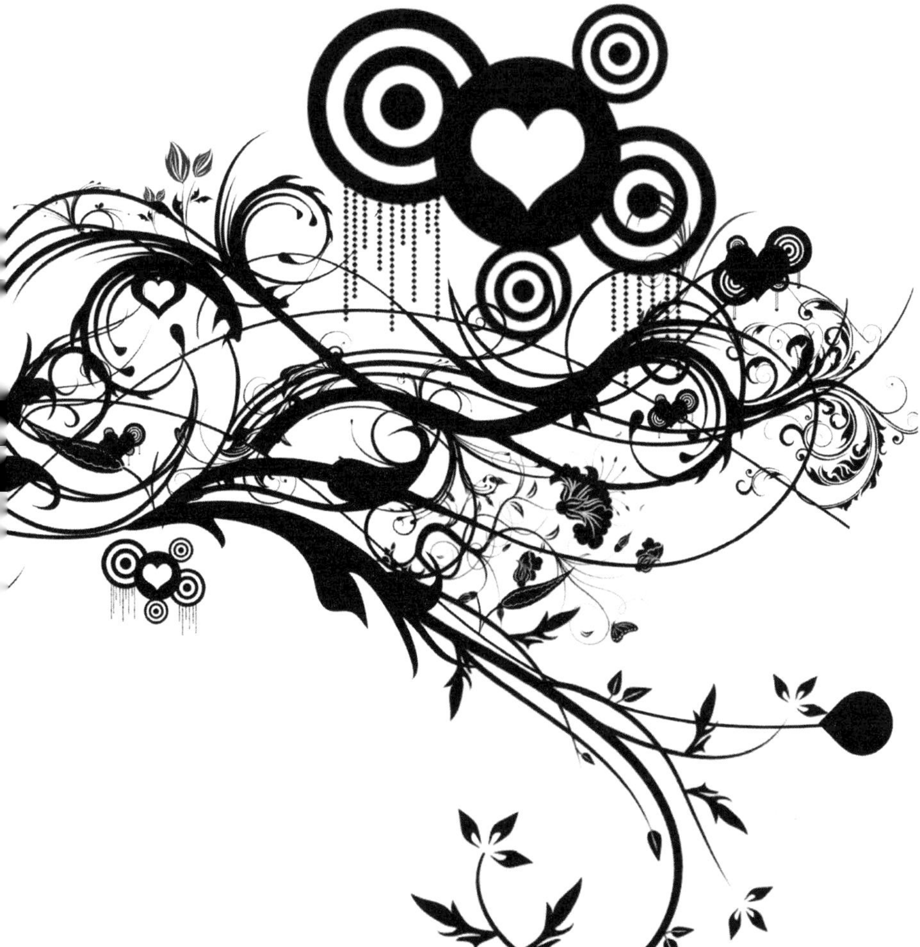

MATURED ONLY

TreNte 32
DeuX

As I lay I pondered Is that my knight I hear calling from beyond? Can it be true that what he sees is reality? Does my stature reveal so much? That another can see my soul Should I heed his call? Am I being pulled into that zone? Of fantasy Where there is no turning back Maybe this is just a ploy To tease me and reel me in Can I taste a little of that knowledge And not get bitten Should I melt into that protective armor? That seems so warm Those eyes that hunger for another's touch That tone that professes safety That mind which holds the secret of understanding Are you my knight? Is it my stature that you seek? Or my soul

MATURED ONLY

TreNte 33
TRois

Soca me baby As I walked in I could feel the heat Bodies gyrating to the melodious sounds of this sweet concoction Of music seducing me, come embrace me, take my hand Let's explore and explode together As I circled the dance floor I was stopped dumfounded by this Smooth honey golden brown brother Moving his waist from side to side Shaking that tight bum while licking those luscious lips Arousing every ounce of my being With his sexy eyes saying soca me baby And I in my mind want to go and partake In this ultimate dance of passion and heat My faucet was dripping over on hot I watched as his hands crept up on her hips As he pulled her into his rhythm Guiding her in time with his Slow nice and easy grove And then fast and rough Just enough to entice and tease me I was done as he moved his hands Ever so slowly to her finger tips Raised her hands in the air Pressed his nose against hers And slowly wined down to the floor and up again I became so moved that my hips took control Ever so slowly beginning to roll His eyes caught mine And suddenly I was a part of Soca me baby Soca me

MATURED ONLY

Have you reached the peak in your relationship? Do you seek more? If you do Have you talked to her about it Do you believe that she can fulfill your needs Does she make you feel special, like a king If so, have you told her? Can you be honest about your feelings? Do you love her till it hurts Do you hold and caress her and let her know it'll be alright How important is she to you Will you catch her if she falls Will you support her Do you miss her till it hurts you know where Is she as beautiful as when you first saw her Can she still captivate your mind Can she make you come by just thinking of her Is she that warm cup of tea, that sooths your soul Is she still your sweetheart Your soul Do you still want her to have your baby Is she the best thing since slice bread When was the last time you told her Do you really know her Does she know you Have you taken the time to Do you hold hands and take long walks Do you hug and kiss as much as possible Does she build you up and encourage you Do you tell her how beautiful she is Do you tell her how proud of her you are Do you take her out and make her feel like the queen she is Does she get a kiss or a rose just because A note or email that says I love or want you Can you be yourself with her What do you do for fun Can you share your true feelings with her If you don't who is If you don't Why not If you don't What are you waiting on If you don't Make life count Be fair Be honest Be you Don't wait until it's too late Live Love Laugh Enjoy life no matter the situation Allow yourself and her to live Share yourself and improve your relationship Life is too short

TreNte 34 QUatRe

MATURED ONLY

TreNte CiNq 35

I miss you As I sit here I can feel Your hands around me I can feel You in me with your legs wrapped around me I can feel The heat of our bodies as they become one I can feel The mind blowing passion of your kiss everywhere I can feel And suddenly I find euphoria

MATURED ONLY

I can accept us not being together And I've been fantasizing the last few hours Just that now you no longer want me It feels like I'm messing with a virgin One that don't know How to open her legs wide enough And I can't penetrate inside The way I want And some how it can be considered rape, But If I continue rubbing it On that secret spot you might just Be turned on enough So it becomes more fun, But is it still ok to take it without asking, Only She won't enjoy it as much as I do Which is disappointing

TreNte SiX

36

MATURED ONLY

I'm looking for a wife That's what he told me Here's my number meet me I'm looking for a wife Words every woman longs to hear You've got my attention I'll meet you Muscular dark chocolate brother With a smile that would melt any heart Go for it Just rolling when eyes meet Bodies pressed that longing awakens Lust My king, my queen Just rolling when My queen, I found a wife I'd like you to be my second Sorry king friends is all I can conquer Ok friend, I know someone that would be perfect for you Filled with delight and curiosity Queen answered Go for it If you're with him I'll always see you We can hang together Here comes the strong person With much brain power unusually calm man The match was made A wonderfully romantic intelligent man It was fun being with him My king arrives prodding and pacing Wanting a piece The game plan I should get what he's getting After the pressure The queen could not bare it Morality sets in The queen bows out of the game Hurting another was not in the plan The true king was the other

trente sept 37

MATURED ONLY

There is a time when you feel that you've lost And somewhere along that dark corridor You see a glimmer of light seeping through A whisper in your ear keeps saying Try until the light goes out And when you see there is no hope Move on, move on Then he came with a dare With that I wanted to blow your mind I wanted to please you like no other Your proposal was a meeting A meeting of trois I agreed not knowing that she was already your prize There was champagne and such To get us in the mood She must care for him as much as I do To give of herself to please him In this afternoon rendezvous' He rented a room one that was warm and comfortable I wanted to back out because I didn't want it But I wanted him It was an afternoon of heat, passion and pleasure Of him with me, with her and her with me I drank to dull the pain The pain of finding there was another Until now I didn't know I drank to drown my emotions I saw his pleasure fulfilled I drank to forget where I was I saw his mind blown The after effect was unexpected I felt nauseous, numb, angry, betrayed and used What was an attempt to get closer Was the beginning on a road to disaster In the name of love

Trente 38 Huit

MATURED ONLY

Trente 39 Neuf

Although we were friends, partners, lovers We came to a junction in our relationship Where no longer We decided to move on You could not accept that I felt violated I pleaded no but you kept on How can someone I trusted Be so disrespectful of my feelings How can you hurt me And feel fulfilled What was once love Is now dead You couldn't keep his hands off me you said You wanted to feel me you said You wanted to touch me you said You wanted to hurt me The passion, the emotion, the hate There was once love Now it's dead

MATURED ONLY

Quarante

It was my birthday I felt sad to the core So sad that I forced myself to sleep Suddenly In the dark I felt A warm soothing feeling on my toes It made me feel so good I was then inoculated with A seducing injection of a hidden potion One that took me to the other side The other side of erotic pleasure One that fulfilled my every need and want And just before I reached my peak There was another Two that set my soul on fire I was taken beyond and back The lights went on What I saw shocked me But I was so high that I didn't want them to stop It was him and her When it was over He exclaimed happy birthday, surprise I couldn't mutter a word Because they took me to a place I've never been But when they left and I landed back on earth I felt dirty, dirty from the taught Dirty from the touch I went to the shower and washed as hard as I could I couldn't get rid of the feel or scent I wondered have I fulfilled his fantasy now Is this what love is Or was this just a passionate encounter

MATURED ONLY

41

QUARA

Love hurts from the bottom of your soul Sometimes I wish it never was Why such emotion exists Why do I have to hurt It's never been kind to me As though I've done something terribly wrong To deserve such pain When will it end How can I stop it Unless in death Where I can't feel or be

MATURED ONLY

I saw him from across the room and all I could think of was how warm his smile made me feel. With each casual hello his smile drew me closer to him and it made me feel so good deep down inside. Each day I looked forward to seeing him, especially on days when I felt down. No one knew but I. As time passed I became his sunshine and that filled me up. I would think of him and hope to see him at all times. With each passing day my need to see him got stronger and it became more. I wanted to feel him deep inside of me. I wanted to smell, touch, lick, and have him scream my name. The problem was that he was taken. I felt that even if it was just one time, it would fulfill that want that need. I just couldn't get him out of my head.

One day he stroked my face and whispered "baby you have the most kissable lips I've ever seen". I giggled, but that was all I needed to hear. Those words made me tingle and gave me goose bumps. There was an instant glow on my face and if you looked real hard you would see the red in my cheeks. What ran through my mind was a series of visions of us in all sorts of positions. The Kama sutra was my mate. I was passionately in like with him, not love but lust. Yes the lust for a handsome chocolate brother, to heal me. He walked with the confidence of a warrior that would slay a woman.

After days of dreaming and wanting, I decided that on this day something was going to happen. I saw him walk by; I stopped and simply asked "you want me"? There was a big smile on his face as if to say are you serious. I just wanted to see his reaction, just a little tease to see where his mind was. We talked about it and decided that it wouldn't be right and someone will get hurt. But we knew that we really did want each other. On that day we kissed and his lips tasted like sweet wine an irresistible sweet wine. I didn't want to stop and neither did he. We knew we had to and that started a series of events that had no end. That kiss turned into a moment of passion that ended with us on a table. When we were done we were both amazed by the passion and greed that we felt. It was sex in heat in the board room. We didn't plan this out loud but we wanted it to happen but when it did we regretted it. We regretted it because it was wrong not because it wasn't good and satisfying it definitely was. We vowed not let it happen again, if we did continue, it would be selfish. That day I left feeling filled. He was deep inside me; I had a piece of him and him a piece of me. His scent, touch, smile and soul I carried with me and each time I thought of him my heart stopped. I felt so close to him that I gasped for air each time I heard his voice or saw his smile.

I went home and asked the lord for forgiveness' because I knew that it was wrong. It was hard to forget because he was very tempting. All I could hear was him saying "this could never happen again" and I agreed totally. This will never happen again. As the days followed I would avoid seeing him but he made a special trip to see me, just to say hi. My heart stopped again for a brief moment and I realized that I had to condition myself not to allow this to happen again.

Each time I stayed away he would pop up with a question. It was very hard and he couldn't understand my actions he felt used, but I know we had an understanding. That didn't change his want for me as he's said he's not finished. Well I was finished. I now often wonder what would have happened. Now that I've gained a little weight, my hair is grey and there are bags under my eyes. Would I still be his sunshine and have the most kissable lips. Would I still be able to get up on that board table and would he still be able to slay me.

To purchase other titles by Jonquille
go to www.emotionalenergy.us

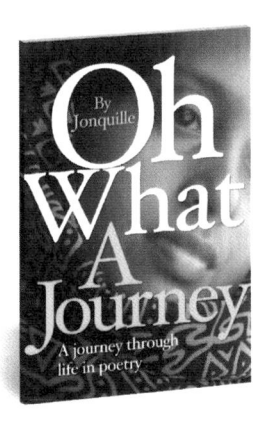

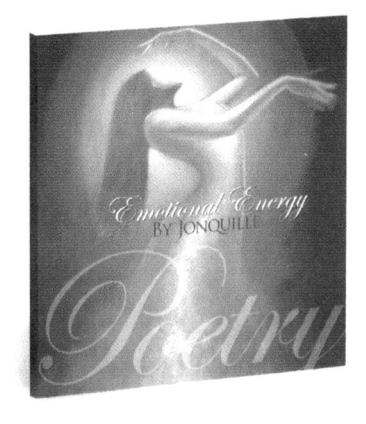

LaVergne, TN USA
25 January 2011
213954LV00001B